...experiencing
home...

...experiencing home...

a guide to finding joy in your home

Jon R. Rentfrow

z.a.j.a.n
PUBLISHING

www.zajanpublishing.com

...experiencing home...

Published by Zajan Publishing
Fort Collins, Colorado   80525

Edited by Margo Cox
Cover by Judith Jones Bertholf

Printed in Canada

FIRST EDITION

ISBN-13   978-0-9818281-0-7

ISBN-10   0-9818281-0-8

Available for purchase at www.zajanpublishing.com

For He who provides all things

Author's Note

     This book was born out of the search for a gift to give my clients when they moved into the newly-built homes I had designed for them. When I started designing homes a number of years ago, I developed a philosophy of "Creating Moods in Individual Spaces." That is, designing a multitude of spaces for people to enjoy during different times of the day and during the different days of their lives. I searched for a gift that complemented my design philosophy, a gift that took my philosophy to the next level. Well, I have ended up creating the gift rather than buying them one.

     To help you understand *...experiencing home...* I thought I might tell you a bit more about me, things that drive the basis and the direction of this book. First, I believe that the God of the Bible is the Creator of life and the Giver of all things. Therefore, everything has a purpose—including our homes. Second, I am a task-oriented type of person. I feel most productive and useful with a list of things to do. If you're also a "list" person, you may be inclined to view this book as just that: something that's easy to fly through and check off the list as done. This book is not about crossing items off a "done" list; it's designed to be a catalyst for you to begin experiencing home in a unique, new way. My hope is that you won't hurry through it, but that you would take your time. Lastly, I am also a "glass half full" kind of a guy. I prefer to look for the positives in most situations and to focus on things for which I am thankful. For example, imagine you are consistently awakened early in the morning by the sound of a woodpecker on the side of your house, or a loud motorcycle thundering down the street. Rather than focusing on how loud or rattling the sound is, the thankful person is glad they have good enough hearing to be able to hear these—some might say—annoying sounds. So you will find in this book the repeated question, "What are you thankful for?" Again, my hope is that you will take the time to give that question some serious thought and meaningful reflection.

I hope you enjoy this time and experience...

Jon

the contents...

the idea...

I have an idea. The idea is this: we are made for home. As a home designer, I venture into people's lives to learn how they live and how they want to live, what they enjoy and what they dislike. Some of my clients' lists are long, some short, but for the most part their lists are all the same. They all want a place that is comfortable, relaxing, and safe. You know what? We all do. We all want a home.

Most of us have a home, but here in the United States we want more and feel we deserve the best of everything; therefore, we plan for the best. We want our houses and, when we want them, we want them now. I am overwhelmed by the number of people who just buy a house on a whim. It seems that if the money is there, why not?

"Is this the home you really want to live in? Or is it the house that is easiest to sell?"

Marianne Cusato, author of "Get Your House Right"

1

We look to upgrade our homes just like we do our television or cell phone because there's a new model out. I have heard so many people say when walking through a $3,000,000.00 show home, "I'll take it when I win the lottery." Would we really be willing to move into a newer model home if we only had the money? Is the lack of money the only thing holding us back? Is it that simple? Would we actually do it? The real question is, is the purchase about improving our home life or is it about changing our image?

We tend to shuffle through houses like we do cars. If we find something new, exciting, and affordable, we buy it, move into it, and then look for something better. Not more than a century ago people kept their homes for generations. There are other cultures around the world who continue to do so even today. I understand that's not always feasible for a number of reasons and I don't expect

"...something inside of me longed for a place to call home."

Jim Daly, Finding Home: An Imperfect Path to Faith and Family

it to change, but what happened to giving our family, our kids, "a place to call home"? What happened to giving them a place to always "come home to," a place where our kids will always feel safe, wanted, and "at home"? We often don't stick around our homes long enough to establish our roots. I understand that families grow, change, and then shrink again, but why must the place we call home change also? The cliché, "your home is where your heart is," makes some sense, but can our hearts really change easily from one house to another? I suggest our hearts move a little slower than our feet or a moving truck.

We dispose of our houses as quickly and often as we do our cars or clothes. Real estate agents are now beginning to refer to existing homes as "used." That term makes a home sound like an old pair of shoes that have lost their treads or jeans with too many holes in the knee. World renowned Architect Robert Stern once said, "Everyone wants the same things in a house—light, coziness, spaces for the family to gather, and other areas that let each person hide out, have a cry, read a book. It doesn't seem like a lot to ask, yet so many of us end up buying the house we hate the least."

Is there a connection between a culture that seems to cherish the family unit less and the loss of significance we place on home? Are we less at peace and more uncomfortable in our own homes? The long-term effects of such a loss are easy to identify, like being so quick to send our elderly to a *home* (strangely enough), and our need to get away from home in order to have a *true* vacation.

Webster's Dictionary defines home as, "*the private living quarters of a person or family.*" Interestingly enough, further definitions of home also found in Webster continuously refer to "*a place that..., a place where...*", etc. Webster tells us, "*a place is any portion of space.*" Space is defined as "*the interval between two or more objects,*" typically walls or furniture, as it relates to homes. An object "*is something that is presented to our senses to excite an emotion.*" I will get to our senses later so let me cut off this running definition.   So where am I going with this? Our homes are personal to our families and to us, yet they are just objects with spaces and places, and oh yeah, *experiences*.

"*A house or apartment is not just a piece of real estate but a place that provides important experiences—that can change your life.*"

Winifred Gallagher, House Thinking

Picture a chilly winter day. The temperature is only twenty-five degrees outside but the sky is clear with the sun shining brightly. The sun casts a ray of warm sunlight onto the wood floor in the south-facing window of your living room and there lies your cat, sleeping the afternoon away. You think to yourself, "Ahh, if only I could waste my day away, right there, on the floor, in the sunlight."

Now imagine coming home from having ridden your bike for a couple of hours. As you enter the house through the garage you are met with the smell of chocolate chip cookies baking in the oven and the sound of the Beatles on the radio. You think to yourself, "This is nice; a good day outside on the bike and now home, where the smells and sounds bring back memories of my childhood. Boy, I wish life was that simple again."

Flash to another scene where you are sitting with your closest friends at the dinner table. The meal is over, the candles are flickering, the music is perfect, you are laughing and joking about something you saw your neighbor do, and you think, "Why can't all my evenings be like this one?"

Do you wish that these types of experiences were more prevalent in your life? Or, that these rooms and spaces were in your home? The spaces and the experiences don't need to be something you wish for. The particular spaces you have in your home are not significant, but the experiences you have in those spaces are. No matter what spaces you have in your home, there are experiences that go along with them. These experiences that all of us have can be special or meaningless, they can be private or public, quiet or loud. Call them what you wish, but the fact is, they are your experiences and yours alone.

Our personal definitions come from what we know and feel, our human perceptions and ideas. For example, I left my childhood home when I moved away to college at the age of 17. To this day, when I tell someone I am going to see my mother for Christmas, I say I am "going home for Christmas." Why do I refer to a place where I do not reside as my home? Hmm...is it because it is a place of comfort, contentment, and safety? A place where memories reside?

Here in Fort Collins, Colorado, the home of Colorado State University, every August, Target and Walmart are fully stocked with all of the things that incoming freshman will need to outfit their dorm rooms. These college students are attempting to make a home out of a 20'x20' room (along with someone else they may not even know). Do you know what? They do it. You know how? They get excited, they plan, they intentionally define spaces; they *live* there. Those little rooms become home to those students because they make the space their own. (However, those same college students will still go home to moms to do their laundry and get a home cooked meal!) Ironically, as soon as they move out of that dorm room there will be a new freshman coming in right behind them with the same intentions.

"Lifestyles are filled with compromise and imperfections, don't let your home be that."

Jane Burdon, *The Comfortable Home*

Some time ago I was in Haiti for a couple of weeks. I was able to see missionaries making the best of what they had in this very poor, third world country. With no running water and limited electricity these missionaries cooked meals that reminded them of home, surrounded themselves with pictures of family, and even hung their national flag on their porch posts. They, like the college students, succeed in making a home wherever they are despite the living conditions and the lack of finances.

American poet Edgar A. Guest is quoted as saying, "It takes a heap o' livin' in a house t' make it home." What a great statement. I'm not sure what a "heap o livin'" is, but it seems to me that "a heap of livin'" has to do with taking the time, making the effort, being patient and deliberate—sort of like creating a heap of leaves for the kids to play in. You have to spend the up front time raking up leaves from all over the yard, dragging them to one specific spot, then methodically circling the heap again and again, trying to make it as tall as possible. Then with one big jump and waving of the arms the heap is destroyed and you begin the circling again. You see? Special times take specific effort. Worthwhile experiences require your intentional attention.

> *A man travels the world over in search of what he needs,*
>
> *and returns home to find it.*
>
> George Moore

A home is no different. To experience our home in a way that brings us joy, it takes being intentional. How do we do this? Do we recognize the place where we live as a home? Do we stop to think about the purpose of our home? Do we live in it the way <u>we</u> were designed to experience it? I believe a sense of *home* is imprinted or woven into our soul. We can see it in the clichés we continue to use, and quite frankly, hold on to. Clichés like "There's no place like home" and "Home is where the heart is" and, of course, "Home sweet home." How is this imprinted? The Creator God has designed us with a sense of home.

Throughout the Bible we can see Him guiding people to the homes He has planned for them. From the very beginning, His plan was to provide a place, a *home*, for Adam and Eve in the Garden of Eden. In the Old Testament, God led the Israelites *home* to the Promised Land. In the New Testament, Jesus Christ established His church for His followers to worship, fellowship and serve together, a church home. Lastly, He has planned for us the ultimate *home*, the final home, with Him. The needs for our homes have changed and the shapes continue to change, but the purpose remains the same. God wants us to experience home.

Along with creating us for home, God the Creator intends for us to experience the things He provides for us—like friends, our jobs and, of course, our *homes*. He wants us to find joy in our daily moments within our home, like hugging our spouses, laughing with our grandchildren, taking a nap in a spot of sunshine, or having that meal with friends. This joy comes from us taking a purposeful look at what we have and making a special effort to appreciate it. This book is aimed at slowing you down so you can contemplate your sense of home with meaning, find the hidden joy within the home you have, and create the experiences that make your house a home.

This book is not about how to design an impressive house or what rooms to remodel to help you enjoy a space better. Rather, this is a guide about how to experience joy within the spaces you already have.

I have an idea...join me...and experience home...

Be still and know that I am God.

Psalm 42:10

the
plan...

So, what's the plan? How do I experience my home? My garage is a pit, the dishes need to be done, I can't lie on the sofa because the unfolded laundry has taken over, and have you seen my son's room?

As a designer, when I begin working with a new home owner I explain to them right off the bat that I will be their guide through the process of designing their home. In the beginning I explain my role, their role, and when the ball is in my court or theirs. As the process continues they count on me to ask the right questions and to steer them towards a completed design. Similarly, I wrote this book to be a guide, to explain the process and to ask the right questions. It is meant to assist you in taking the first steps on the journey to experiencing your home. Keep in mind that your role will take effort. It also means that it will take some time (just like a leaf pile.) Following this guide will be a time of discovery and a time for reflecting on the experiences of home in your past and what you want your experiences of home to be now. I hope you will appreciate this guide as much as my clients have appreciated being led through the design process.

This book will guide you on the journey through your home one space at a time. Throughout this guide you will be asked different questions based on the specific room/space in which you find yourself. Questions like: how significant is this space to your everyday life? Or, what do the sounds of this room stir in you? Your journey will begin on the front porch, meander through the house, and culminate somewhere in the backyard.

Slight detour here. Whenever you enter a home for the first time, whether it's, old, new, being built or whether you know the owner or not, you should always enter through the front door. Homes are designed to be experienced in a given order, and the front porch and entryway are meant to be the first impression; not the garage or the mud room. There you go, my little 'Home Design 101' lecture for the day.

You might choose to experience specific legs of the journey at different times of the day, different days of the week, and different times of the year—all of which might affect the experience in any given room. I have had clients request a formal living room just to have a place for their Christmas tree. They recognize that the room won't be used much, but those few weeks around Christmas are significant enough to justify it for them. Obviously, attempting to experience that room in August is completely different than in December.

This book will also serve as a journal. Journals are valuable tools that enable us to write down the important moments in our lives we hope not to forget. When journaling, we take time to slow down and think, or meditate. There are many terms used today to describe how we go about meditating—terms like contemplation, ponder, or even "follow your muse." I like to use the word reflect. Why? It makes me think of looking in the mirror and seeing things that are actually there. Not just hopes and dreams, and spiritual possibilities, but the reality of my life. Reality includes both good and bad memories, our accomplishments and our failures, as well as our current circumstances. These are all things worth reflecting on as you journal throughout these pages.

As you walk through this guide, my desire is for you to be encouraged and better equipped to find in your present home a place where God has planned for you to be and to experience the joy of that place. I believe experiencing your home will cause you to feel some of the joy God intends for you on earth. I hope it will stir in you an appreciation for what you already have—even if your home has an outdated kitchen, out-of-style paint colors, a squeaky floor, an old sofa and the garage is full of everything but a car. Rather than feeling the need to sell and move on to the next house or figure out how to remodel the kitchen (although you do need to clean your garage!), I want you to sit back, grab a cup of coffee, be still, reflect, and experience.

Ultimately, my hope is that the adventure of this journey won't end for you when you reach the final page, but rather that you will pick this guide up again someday at another time and experience the journey again and again.

> *"What really makes a house a home is how successfully it supports our daily activities and it expresses and nurtures our best thoughts, memories, feelings and patterns of behavior—our way of life."*
>
> *Winifred Gallagher, House Thinking*

the
perspective...

Let me take you through a little exercise. By exercise I don't mean stretching and jumping jacks, but an example to prove a point. To someone watching, you might look a bit silly doing this so take a second and make sure you're alone. First, point your right pointer finger in the air, above your head. Second, begin to move your hand and finger in a clockwise fashion. Now, while you continue the circular motion and you keep your palm pointing away from you, move your hand down to eye level. Next, without stopping the circular motion and still keeping your palm pointing away, (and not towards the ground) move your hand and finger down to your waist area. What do you notice? Has anything changed? Is your finger now moving in a counter-clockwise direction? Did you actually change the direction your finger was going, or just how you view it? You see, your perspective has changed.

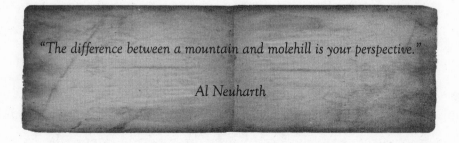

"The difference between a mountain and molehill is your perspective."

Al Neuharth

Webster's Dictionary tells us that *"perspective is the evaluation of events according to a particular way of looking at them."* In other words, perspective is the difference between the way we view or perceive things and the way they actually are. You see, one's perspective is personal, individual, and obviously not right or wrong. Let's say there is a car accident in the middle of an intersection. Four people, one on each opposing street corner, see the accident and give a report of what they saw. All four individuals have just witnessed the same event, yet all may give what appear to be contradictory statements. Is anyone lying? Or, are they simply explaining what they saw from their individual perspective, therefore slightly different? The latter would account for the apparent discrepancies.

What is the relevance of perspective to our homes? Well, we all view the rooms in our homes differently. Some may appreciate a bright, sunlit room; others may say it's too bright. You might think your front porch is the perfect size for a large swing and, therefore, a place to relax under a blanket with your spouse. Your neighbor's may view your porch as ugly, a waste of space and, most importantly, they don't care for the public displays of affection. This can be illustrated by a couple with whom I once worked. I'll refer to them as Bob and Susan. On Sunday Bob loves to watch his favorite football team downstairs in front of the TV in his most comfortable chair and under his softest blanket. His wife Susan's perspective is a bit different. To Susan, "The TV room, ugh! He just goes down there to hide and veg in front of that box, and then he yells at it all day long." To Susan it's a room of wasted time and energy. As I mentioned earlier, there is no right or wrong here. They just have very different perspectives.

> *"Humans know what does or doesn't feel right. I can't sing in tune, but when I watch American Idol, I know when someone else is out of tune. We all know when a house doesn't feel right."*
>
> *Marriane Cusato, author of "Get Your House Right"*

Our different perspectives are influenced by what we view as important. What's important to you? Time with your spouse? Or a walk with your dog? Maybe some quiet time by yourself? It's definitely not the same for all of us. I sure wish a bike ride in the fresh air gave me energy at the end of the day, but it doesn't. Personally, spending time with my kids is very important. What's important to us dictates how we live in our homes and how we use specific spaces. For instance, my family has different perspectives as to what is fun on our swing set. My oldest son Nicholas swings as high and crazily as possible while singing and yelling, then jumps off the swing in mid-air.. My youngest son Zekiah likes to lie on the swing on his belly staring at the ground humming, slightly moving around. I, on the other hand, prefer to rock calmly back-n-forth on the swing quietly. My perspective is one of relaxation, Nicholas' is one of excitement. They view the swing as important, me—not so much. Each of us has a different perspective of the swing set based on the importance we place on it.

> *"Think carefully about the time we spend in our homes, our day-to-day tasks, and the activities that we enjoy and find important."*
>
> Jane Burdon, The Comfortable Home

Our perspectives are also influenced by the five senses God has created within us. In our homes, certain smells or sounds are definitive to certain spaces.

For instance, to a friend of mine the smell of car oil in the garage reminds him of time spent with his father working on the car. To me, it smells like trouble and anxiety brewing. Perhaps the sound of popcorn popping evokes feelings of comfort or fun. The sound of a dog barking elicits yet other feelings and emotions. In one combination or another, our five senses give us the ability to respond to the experiences God gives us.

Our overall perspective may be that our lives are busy, chaotic, stressful, and even too full of "giving ourselves to others." We may think that if the clothes were folded sooner (and put away), the kids had fewer activities, the yard didn't need to be mowed, or we didn't have work to do at home that life would be better, slower, more peaceful. Although this may be true, God's perspective is a bit different than ours. I don't believe if God were to instantly improve our domestic lives He would give all of us a chauffeur, a nanny and a four-star kitchen that self cleans. Instead, He would clean our hearts, slow us down, and get us to approach our lives and homes from a different perspective—His. God's perspective is for us to experience peace, love, hope, and as I have mentioned before, joy. As we learn more about God we begin to understand His perspective. Eventually, we begin to see the pointer finger from the same perspective He does.

the
experience...

The simple fact is that we need to feel more at home in our homes. In her book *House Thinking*, Winifred Gallagher quotes an environmental psychologist by the name of Lynne Manzo, who makes a very true and simple statement. "The important element in how our past homes affect our present ones is not the places themselves, but our experience in them." With this statement as a basis, you now get to take your first step of this journey.

I want you to try and remember your childhood home. I realize there is a strong possibility that you lived in a number of different homes while growing up; I want you to choose only one of them. Strangely, we remember our childhood homes in very interesting ways don't we? Sometimes it's by the color of the house (the little blue house) or the street name it was located on (house on Gunnison). Sometimes it's by the size or age, or, believe it or not, we sometimes name our childhood homes based on one event that happened at that house (the tornado house)—a significant experience you might say.

Take a few minutes and think about the floor plan of that house. Don't worry about exact sizes and proportions, but think through which rooms were connected to other rooms and where there were windows and doors. I want you to begin to draw that floor plan on the grid paper provided on the following pages.

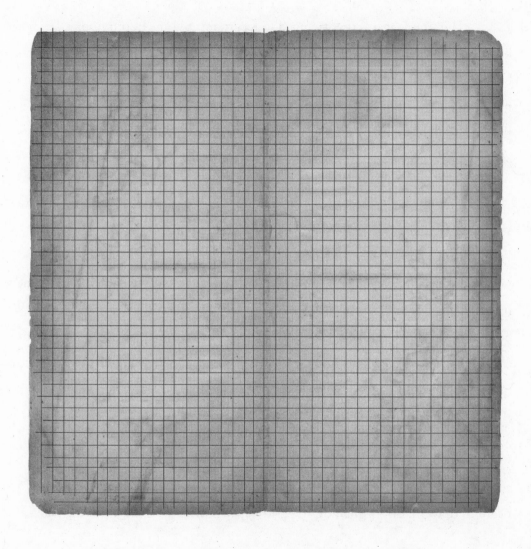

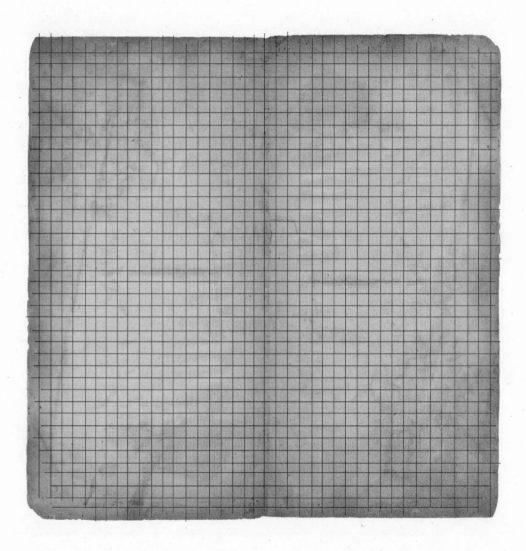

I want you to label the rooms and any other significant details you might remember. You might remember where the TV always was, or where your bed was, or even the details of the kitchen. If there is something special about the backyard or the driveway, then sketch that as well.

Next, if you can get over the quality of your sketch, I want you to write down the memories that this stirs in you. Think through things like: where did you spend most of your time and why? Where in the home did you feel the safest? Which rooms were the brightest, the quietest? What color were most of the rooms? Spend some time reflecting. No need to rush.

_____

_____

_____

_____

_____

_____

_____

_____

_____

_____

These reflections may include both good memories and bad memories, which is okay because they are all relevant to how you view that childhood home. Was it easier to remember the floor plan of that particular home or, to recall the actual experiences within the home? I think for most people, the memories are strong and the specifics of the house are few and are far between. I remember staying at a beach house with my family in Southwest Florida a number of years ago. I don't remember the house at all; yet I have a vivid memory of playing football on the beach with my brother and cousins, my uncles, and most importantly, my father. This experience is very significant to me because it was the last thing I did in the form of sports with my father before he passed away.

Do all children have the same experiences in their respective childhood homes? Absolutely not. There are some similarities though. I had a good, healthy and memorable childhood. But, as a child, I was afraid to get out of my bed at night unless I could do it without touching the floor (otherwise the 500 slithering, hungry snakes would get me). Others are so afraid of the dark they go diving into their bed once the light is turned off. For most of us, our childhood beds were a safe zone, a refuge from all outside noises and imagined monsters in the closet. Obviously, our individual childhood experiences will differ. I recognize some may have such horrible memories they would prefer not to recollect those experiences. Whether the memories are good or bad, they are significant. These childhood memories have shaped our lives.

> *If there are significantly bad experiences in your childhood that you as an adult have not been able to deal with, I would encourage you to search out resources that can help you. First, I would encourage you to pray to the God that heals, strengthens and gives real hope. Also, I have listed some books and websites in "the sources" chapter that may be able to help you. Take a look.*

The next stop in this journey is to reflect on your existing home. What experiences are you having in your present home? Without taking a tour of your home first, I want you to sit in one place and create a list of the rooms/spaces in your home. I want you to list only the spaces in your home that you like. Not including the why (yet); just make the list.

_____   _____

_____   _____

_____   _____

_____   _____

_____   _____

Now make a list of rooms you don't like. Again, don't analyze why, just do it quickly. (You can't say your basement. That is an entire level of the house and that's a cop-out. If there is a specific space within your basement, I suppose that would be acceptable.)

_____   _____

_____   _____

_____   _____

_____   _____

Now I want you to write down the one space you like the most.

_____

Why do you think you like it the most?   Is it because it's the most comfortable (the best light and temperature)? Is it because of where the room is located (the most accessible to where everyone else always is)?

_____

_____

_____

_____

_____

_____

_____

_____

_____

Which space do you like the least?

_____

You know what? The temperature of the room is highly significant to how it ultimately feels. A room that is too hot will feel stuffy and sticky. A room that is too cold will never allow you to relax. You will constantly be shifting around, attempting to get comfortable unless you are underneath a down comforter or in your bed with your toes comfortably warm.

Why do you think you like it the least? Is it always cold? Is it too isolated for you? Is it uncomfortable?

_____

_____

_____

_____

_____

_____

_____

Have you ever thought about the fact that certain spaces are introverted or extroverted? The type of person you are will help determine why a space feels nice or not. Are you an extrovert, or an introvert? Our bedrooms feel introverted; it seems weird when others are in our bedrooms. Frankly, most of us feel uncomfortable going into someone else's bedroom. Kitchens, on the other hand (these days especially), are extroverted. Like many of my clients tell me, "The kitchen is the place where everyone hangs out," and kitchens are definitely designed for their showmanship. You will typically feel more comfortable in the places that align with your personality.

It goes without saying, of course, that an experience you have had in any given space will have influence on whether or not you like it. Is it a great space because that is where you always have coffee and read the paper on Saturday mornings? Or, maybe it's a bad space because that's where you last saw a close friend that moved **away**? Then again, depending on your perspective, maybe that's a good place because it is where you last saw a close friend **just before** they moved away.

> *"For most of us, 'living well' begins and ends with the private world we create for ourselves and share with friends."*
>
> *Pottery Barn:* HOME

Many of our experiences are significant because we enjoyed them with someone else. So maybe you like your front porch the most because that is where you relax with your wife on Friday nights and talk about your week.

Now we continue the journey as we consider the individual spaces of your home. When you find yourself staring at ugly upholstery on the sofa or outdated tile in the foyer, look past it. Don't get caught up with the furnishings and finishes of any given space. They are not important to this journey because any beauty, or lack thereof, is not significant to the experience.

One last note, I may attempt to guide you through a space you don't have in your home. You may skip it or change it, do whatever you wish. The important factor is that you take the time on the spaces you do have.

"There's a world of difference between having a roof over your head at night and being at home."

Jim Daly, Finding Home: An Imperfect Path to Faith and Family

the
front porch...

The front porch is the first thing people see when they approach your home. It's the space where people stand as they wait for you to answer the door. It's where you sit and watch your kids ride their bikes or talk with your neighbor about the latest news on the block. The front porch has many significant roles, but in today's culture these roles are being lost. It used to be the place we entered when we came home and the place where dad would see his family waiting for him as he returned home. Nowadays most of us tend to enter our homes through our garage. The garage door opener opens the overhead door, we drive in, shut the overhead door behind us, and walk into the house the back way. I suppose it's one of the "Laws of Convenience" we Americans love.

Architecturally, the front porch has great power of influence, either positively or negatively and I'm sure you have created your own opinions on such a matter. I have a client who said something I love, "It's very important how people experience our home, even though they may not be coming to see us."

> *"The best thing about a front porch is the transition between the home and the yard, and the welcoming connection to the neighborhood."*
>
> *Builder Magazine, May 2006*

What effect does entering your home through your garage have on your daily life?

_____

_____

_____

_____

_____

_____

_____

How does your front porch feel to you? Loud or quiet, dark or bright, spacious or scary?

_____

_____

_____

_____

_____

What finishes does your front porch have—wood, concrete, stone, painted siding?

_____

_____

Do you think those materials have any effect on how the porch feels to you? Like what?

_____

_____

_____

_____

Do you prefer to be alone when on the porch or is it the place where you go to spend time with others?

_____

_____

_____

As you sit on your porch and look at the street you live on, what do you remember? Neighborhood block parties? Baseball in the street? Watching your grandchildren play with other neighbor kids?

_____

_____

_____

_____

_____

_____

_____

_____

_____

I remember a small group of friends coming over and standing on our porch, singing to our family, to encourage us. As I stand on my porch I am reminded of friendship, fellowship and the everlasting memories those friends gave me.

How much does your front porch create a "security buffer" for your home from the outside world?

_____

_____

_____

_____

If you sit on your porch do you feel too exposed to anyone who might pass by? Or, do you savor the opportunity of talking with a passerby?

_____

_____

_____

What is the favorite part and/or worst part about your front porch?

_____

_____

_____

We are opening our homes to the outdoors like never before. If you are looking for a living room outside, try that good-ol' American treasured and cherished front porch.

What are you thankful for in your front porch?

_____

_____

_____

_____

_____

_____

_____

_____

_____

_____

My people will live in peaceful dwelling places, in secure homes,

in undisturbed places of rest.

Isaiah 32:18

the
entryway...

First impressions are highly significant to our life's experiences. The entryways into our homes are the means for that first impression for all who enter. We put in our entryway the things that matter to us, the things we want to display in order to convey who we are; items like family pictures, framed diplomas or a meaningful sculpture. In my family's entryway we have our family mission statement hung on the wall. Immediately upon entering our home we want people to know what our family is about and what our home is used for.

Also, the size of your entryway doesn't matter. Your front door may open right into your living room or your entryway may be the size of a two-car garage. Either way, they have the same function, to move people in and out of your home.

A good entry tells you that you've left the mad world behind for a private haven and invites the expectation of pleasures to come.

Winifred Gallagher, House Thinking

What do you have on the walls in your entryway? Are they things that are important to you? Why?

_____

_____

_____

_____

_____

What do you wish was in your entryway? Why?

_____

_____

_____

_____

_____

_____

Stand in your entryway with your front door behind you. What do you see?

_____

_____

_____

_____

_____

List some of the people who have been in your entryway.

_____ _____ _____

_____ _____ _____

Why were some of them there? Anything life-altering (positively or negatively)?

_____

_____

_____

_____

_____

_____

Entryways are about coming and going for you and your family. It's also the place in which visitors leave your home.

What is the most joyful goodbye you have had at your front door?

_____

_____

_____

_____

_____

How about the most sorrowful?

_____

_____

_____

_____

_____

_____

What are you thankful for in your entryway?

_____

_____

_____

_____

_____

_____

_____

_____

the
study...

As I begin to work with new clients, designing their home for them, I always spend some very intentional time discussing their study/den/office. I attempt to clarify how they intend to use the space. I want to design for them a space that supports the way they really live. There is a significant difference between the traditional den where dad escapes to read or where Ward Clever had the boys come in to talk with him and the kind of space where someone may run a house painting business. Not only do these two spaces function differently, but a lot of times they may be located in different parts of the home. The den is typically near the front part of the house, a rather formal space with french doors and sometimes a fireplace. On the other hand, the working office tends to be near the back of the home, where one's guests won't see it. Today, we often refer to either the den or the office as the study, which is how I'll refer to it.

Who uses the study in your home? Is it for the entire family, or just for one specific person?

_____

_____

_____

_____

What are you inspired to do in the study? Read? Work? Sleep?

_____

_____

_____

_____

_____

_____

_____

Reflect on the history of this study. Have you seen its needs evolve? Perhaps it's changed from a traditionally decorated den to a bill paying center.

_____

_____

_____

_____

_____

_____

_____

_____

_____

     Now, reflect on your experiences in former studies; the one you grew up in, or maybe the one where you asked an important question of your future father-in-law.

_____

_____

_____

_____

_____

_____

_____

_____

Lay down on the floor in your study (if there is not enough room to lay down, find a place to sit).

What do you see on the ceiling?

_____

_____

_____

Does this new perspective change how you feel about the study?

_____

_____

_____

"Natural light keeps you energized and inspired."

Pottery Barn: HOME

What do you hear? Is your study quiet or chaotic?

_____

_____

_____

_____

_____

What are you thankful for about your study?

_____

_____

_____

_____

_____

_____

_____

_____

_____

the
living room...

Do you have a living room, a family room, both, or a great room? (A great room is essentially one living space, not necessarily as big as the other two combined, but usually a bit larger than just one of them.) Generally, our homes have a casual living space separate from a formal living space. A more modern home typically has a great room. Ultimately, call it what you want. What do I want you to do if you have both a living room and a family room? Consider both, but do them individually. My guess is that you live in them quite differently.

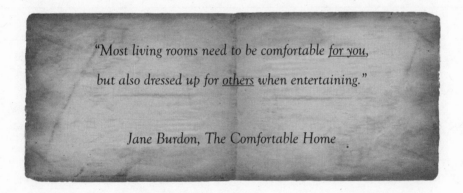

"Most living rooms need to be comfortable <u>for you</u>, but also dressed up for <u>others</u> when entertaining."

Jane Burdon, The Comfortable Home

The living room is the place where you sit with others and talk, perhaps watch TV, celebrate holidays, and if you're like me, take a nap. The living room is probably the most widely used space in your home because you use it alone, with family or with friends; therefore, the experiences are probably broad and uniquely different from one another. My guess is that where you are positioned in your living room influences the experience as well—such as sitting on the hearth, which is often a focal point during the cold months. Or, maybe playing a game of Scrabble on the floor.

Search your memory for all of the different ways you have used your living room.

_____

_____

_____

Would you consider your living room to be large or small?

_____

_____

Does its size prevent you from doing something you wish you could? Like what? (i.e., too small to host an office party or too large to take a cozy nap?)

_____

_____

_____

What kinds of things happen in your living room that happen nowhere else in your home?

_____

_____

_____

_____

Do you like to entertain others in your home? Why or why not?

_____

_____

_____

_____

Try to remember a time when you had guests in your home, some of which you did not know very well. What was it like? Fulfilling, stressful, eventful, maybe all of the above?

_____

_____

_____

_____

_____

_____

_____

Where do you celebrate the holiday seasons?

_____

_____

If applicable, where do you like to place your Christmas tree? Do you like to place the tree where only you see it, or do you like your neighbors to see it in the window? Why?

_____

_____

_____

_____

_____

> It seems like in my home, when the Christmas tree is up,
>
> it's the focal point of our family interaction.
>
> My wrestling matches with the boys move to the foot of the tree.
>
> Story times at night are moved to the sofa next to the tree,
>
> where the soft white lights set the mood.
>
> I am reluctant to turn the tree lights off as I go to bed.
>
> I sort of want the mood to continue and to spend some time alone.

What is the favorite seat in your living room? Where do most people choose to sit?

_____

_____

_____

_____

_____

_____

What does the furniture arrangement of the living room indicate about its purpose? Does the room have a focal point?

_____

_____

_____

Think through your most memorable time with family in your living room. What makes it the best versus some other time?

_____

_____

_____

What can you see from your living room? Other spaces in your home? How about the view out of the windows?

_____

_____

_____

_____

Most of us watch television in our living rooms. Whether it's movies, sports, or a favorite sitcom, we all tend to have a preference. What do you like to watch on television?

_____

_____

_____

Do not forget to entertain strangers, for by so doing some people

have entertained angles without knowing it.

Hebrews 13:2

What are you most thankful for in your living room?

_____

_____

_____

_____

_____

the
dining area...

Is your main dining area formal or casual? What makes the difference? Well, the formal dining room typically entails a defined space set aside specifically for dining engagements. The casual dining area tends to be extremely versatile. It's used for eating, homework, sewing, and, in our home, everything we carry in from the garage when we come home. It seems that these days the casual dining area is home base, the hub of all that is going on in the home.

> *Our dining table has pretty much been broken up into thirds.*
> *One third is the drop off area for everything we bring home.*
> *The second third is where school is done, and the*
> *final third is where we actually eat. We haven't drawn*
> *lines on the table (yet) to define the thirds, but some of*
> *the large piles are pretty definitive.*

This chapter will deal with both the formal and the casual dining spaces because they are traditionally used much differently. So if one or more of the questions doesn't apply to you, maybe a home you grew up in applies. If not, skip the question all together.

List all of the things for which your casual dining space is used, then, number them in order of most important.

_____

_____

_____

_____

_____

Do you think the others in your household would agree with the way you have ranked your list? How might theirs differ?

_____

_____

_____

Which of the two spaces do you prefer? The casual or the formal? Why?

_____

_____

_____

_____

If you have both the formal and casual spaces and have guests over, where do you tend to eat with them? Why?

_____

_____

_____

_____

Do you enjoy having others over for dinner? Who was your most memorable dinner guest? Why?

_____

_____

_____

_____

What was served at that meal? What tastes or smells do you recall?

_____

_____

_____

_____

> "Bringing together friends and family is one of life's greatest joys and privileges...mixing old friends with new."
>
> Pottery Barn: HOME

Formal dining rooms are often decorated uniquely within the home. Even though someone may have a contemporary style of décor in the rest of their home, you still might see their great-grandmother's (very Victorian) dining room set in the formal dining room. It's typically a family heirloom that dictates this uniqueness and formal dining rooms seem to be the place where these heirlooms are kept and often displayed.

What items do you have in your formal dining room? (furniture and decorations)

_____

_____

_____

If you have an heirloom or other special object in the room, sit at the table and spend some time reflecting on the significance of that item(s). How does it make you feel?

_____

_____

_____

_____

_____

_____

_____

Formal dining rooms are also the place for celebrations. Whether it's Thanksgiving, an anniversary or a baptism, the formal dining room seems to be the most appropriate space to celebrate.

What is the most memorable celebration in your formal dining room? Who was present?   Again, what was served? What mattered most? Was it the food, the people, or the reason for the celebration?

_____

_____

_____

_____

_____

_____

> *"One of the most iconic and enduring images of home is that of the whole family gathered around the table, laughing and chatting."*
>
> *Pottery Barn:* HOME

The lighting in a dining space is extremely important. I guess we really want to know what our food looks like, or how much the fine china glistens from the high-powered halogen bulbs. However, candles are usually on the table nearby. Candles are the essence of warmth and timelessness in our homes.

Do you prefer bright lights or soft candlelight while you eat? Does the occasion matter? (e.g., birthday versus anniversary)

_____

_____

_____

_____

What are you thankful for in either one, or both, of your dining areas?

_____

_____

_____

_____

_____

_____

the
kitchen...

How do you use your kitchen? Is it just for cooking or is it where most of your family conversations are held? Today, the kitchen is without question the center of the home. Again and again I hear from my clients, "There needs to be plenty of room around the kitchen island because it's where everyone congregates." Since it's typically the center of the family's activities there's always multi-tasking going on—like cooking, talking about the day, checking homework, paying the bills, etc.

I have this image in my head of most men in America arriving home from work finding their wife preparing dinner in the kitchen. He leans against the counter as he loosens his tie and shoelaces. He asks how the day went at home and she's curious how the important meeting went at work. Maybe this is too much of a *Norman Rockwell* painting, but I think there is a lot of truth to the general idea. The kitchen definitely seems to be the place where we have our most significant conversations and reconnect with our families after going different directions all day long.

Other than cooking, of course, what kinds of things do you do in your kitchen?

_____

_____

_____

How about conversations? What do you typically talk about with others when in your kitchen?

_____

_____

_____

Reflect on a significant conversation you have had in your kitchen. Was it one-of-a-kind or typical?

_____

_____

_____

_____

When I designed my mother's home, one thing she wanted was a large

(one-level) island in her kitchen for serving large buffet dinners.

She enjoys having others over and really wanted a place to put the food,

the plates, etc. Now that her grandboys are getting older, however, the

island has taken on a new responsibility. With its three bar stools, that

island is now where the boys instinctively sit every morning we are there

for breakfast. The island has become part of the kitchen ritual; a

place and a ritual that's become familiar, comfortable, and fun.

As long as she lives where she does, the island will continue to

have a dual function—parties and a place for the grandboys to line

up like little owls on a fence. And you know what? One day,

the boys, my mom—all of us—will have lots of

wonderful memories and stories to tell about "grandma's island".

How does your kitchen relate to the rest of your home? Is it central, in the corner, etc? Does its position in the home have relevance to how you use it? Why or why not?

_____

_____

_____

When designing a home I always attempt to put the kitchen and breakfast area where it will receive the morning sunlight. The warmth of the sun in the morning is energizing and encouraging for the new day. The morning sun should also remind us of the faithfulness of God as He provides another day for us to experience. For me, it's the place for that ever-so-important first glass of orange juice. I always encourage my clients to entertain the idea of windows rather than upper cabinets in their kitchen to enable the sunlight to have an effect.

Is the light in your kitchen predominantly natural or artificial? Which do you prefer? Why?

_____

_____

_____

Is the kitchen a part of your morning ritual? If so, what part? Why or why not?

_____

_____

_____

_____

Do you have things stuck to your fridge? Like what?

_____

_____

Why these things? What do they mean to you?

_____

_____

_____

Our kitchens also seem to tie many memories together from our childhoods. It might be a food recipe you were taught that you still enjoy. Maybe it was some science experiment done at the kitchen sink that convinced you that you would someday be an astronaut.

> *"Cooking is at once child's play and adult joy. And cooking*
>
> *done with care is an act of love.*
>
> *Craig Claiborne*

Who taught you to cook?

_____

_____

What's your favorite thing to cook? Where did you learn the recipe?

_____

_____

_____

As a child did you ever do a science experiment in your kitchen? What was it?

_____

_____

_____

Are there certain smells in your kitchen that stir specific memories for you? Like what?

_____

_____

_____

_____

What are you most thankful for in your childhood kitchen?

_____

_____

_____

_____

What are you most thankful for in your present kitchen?

_____

_____

_____

_____

_____

the
play area...

Do you have a play area in your home? Many people don't, so I'll try to use as broad a definition as I can. If you have young kids you may have a play room full of cars, dolls, train tracks, etc. If you have older kids the play area may be where they play the latest video game system. As an adult you may have a place that is set aside for billiards, ping pong, or even a movie theater. For the sake of this discussion, let's group all of them into the play area definition.

Because of this broad definition, the list of where the play area might be is long. Again, if it's a space for younger kids, it's probably somewhere near where the adults typically are. For older kids, their play area is probably as far away from the adults as possible. I have found over the years that the adults play areas are all over the place. Some are in the basement, above the garage, or even in a separate building detached from the house. No matter their location, we have these kinds of spaces to relax and enjoy ourselves.   Most of the time we are enjoying these spaces with someone else.

> *"The ornament of a house is the friends who frequent it."*
>
> *Ralph Waldo Emerson*

What kind of play area(s) do you have? If you need to, stretch my definition even further.

_____

_____

_____

_____

What kinds of things do you like to do as recreation in your home?

_____

_____

_____

What kind of people do you have over to enjoy these spaces with you?

_____

_____

_____

_____

_____

In our playroom just off the kitchen is a very large, stuffed, blue pillow. We, very cleverly, call it "the big pillow," because it's about six feet in diameter. That pillow is the place for epic pillow fights, tickle wrestling, and even naps. We also have a space downstairs where we have set up the TV for the best possible movie experience. Two different spaces, two different uses, but both we consider to be play areas.

What sounds remind you of times in your play area?

_____

_____

_____

How about smells?

_____

_____

_____

I find it interesting that we initially go to our play areas to enjoy ourselves by playing games or watching a movie. However, as the evening continues, the play area seems to be the space where we hang out, relax and have long conversations. Our play areas seem to change from loud and crazy to quiet and peaceful.

Reflect on a time in your play area that means a lot to you.

_____

_____

_____

_____

_____

_____

_____

_____

_____

_____

What are you most thankful for in your play area(s)?

_____

_____

_____

_____

_____

_____

_____

_____

_____

_____

_____

_____

the
bedroom...

Do you think of your bedroom as an introverted or extroverted space? I would argue that in general our bedrooms are introverted. Why? For the most part, we don't want anybody in our bedrooms that we don't know very well. I don't think it has anything to do with the unmade bed or laundry all over the floor, but more about intimacy and security.

> *"We should feel secure in our bedrooms...it's interesting that scared people in movies always run to their bedrooms."*
>
> Jane Burdon, *The Comfortable Home*

What's interesting is that as I design master suites I continue to make them bigger, nicer and more of a show piece, but it doesn't seem to change the expectations of the owner. They still want their privacy and safety. They still want a cozy and comfortable place to escape.

How do you view your bedroom? Introverted or extroverted? Why?

_____

_____

_____

What things do you have on your walls? Would you consider these things to be private or public?

_____

_____

_____

_____

_____

Is your bedroom generally clean or dirty? How do think that alters your mood?

_____

_____

_____

> *Design 101, again. Your bedroom will look larger if upon entering the room you see the foot of the bed. The bedroom will look smaller if you walk in and see a side of the bed.*

As you stand in the doorway of your bedroom. What is your perception of the space?

_____

_____

_____

Now stand in the opposite corner of the bedroom, looking back towards the door. Is the overall perception any different? How so?

_____

_____

_____

_____

Currently, the popular design trends within master bedrooms/suites are defined sitting areas, fireplaces, and even direct access to exercise and massage rooms. Our bedrooms are our retreats, the place we long to return to, the place where we look to leave behind the stresses of the day. I don't know about you, but no matter where I travel or how long I'm there, I'm always ready to get home and sleep in my own bed.

Other than sleeping and intimate contact with your spouse, what other things do you do in your bedroom?

_____

_____

_____

_____

Do you like to nest in your bed (read a book, watch TV, hide out)? Why?

_____

_____

_____

_____

"NEST- A snug, comfortable, or cozy residence or situation;

a retreat, or place of habitual resort"

How relevant is sunlight in your bedroom? (Does it wake you up in the morning, or help you nap on Sunday afternoon?)

_____

_____

_____

_____

_____

_____

Do you get direct sunlight on your bed? Do you like that, or not? Why?

_____

_____

_____

_____

_____

What is the best thing about your bedroom?

_____

_____

_____

_____

_____

_____

_____

the
bath area...

Let's move on to the bath area. You may be asking why I don't use the term "bathroom." Well, in some houses there is much more to it than just the place you shower and brush your teeth. Without question, there is a vast difference in bath areas between any two houses you may choose, or even between individual bath areas within a given home. What makes so much of ...*experiencing home...* interesting is that there are experiences to be had in small or large, generic or glamorous, even traditional or modern bath areas.

We see the importance of the bath area revealing itself in a number of places. For one, bath areas are being designed larger and more extravagantly. In larger homes, the bath area may include the closet and dressing area and even a coffee area. Secondly, it's evident that advertisements in magazines or on television that are related to relaxation, resting or even romance are often staged in the bath area.

How would you describe your bath area? Generic, glamorous, intimate, etc.?

_____

_____

_____

What makes it that way? The size? The amenities (or lack thereof)?

_____

_____

_____

_____

Think through some of the other bath areas you have been in before that you have really liked. What are the key differences between those areas and yours? (It might be things like the size, the layout, the daylight, the colors, or even the scent of candles or linens.)

_____

_____

_____

_____

Yes, bath areas are the places where we do many utilitarian things, but they are also a place to relax and refresh.

> *"What I dream of is an art of balance, of purity and serenity*
>
> *devoid of troubling or depressing subject matter—a*
>
> *soothing, calming influence on the mind."*
>
> *Henri Matisse*

Is your bath area a place where you relax? Why or why not?

_____

_____

_____

Are you typically "in and out" of the bath area? (Just getting ready in the morning and moving on with your day.)

_____

_____

_____

_____

How much time do you spend in your bath area? In your opinion, is it too much or too little?

_____

_____

_____

_____

Our bath area is pretty limited in space, especially when all five of us are standing in front of the same mirror and sink. So needless to say, we are "in and out" pretty quick in our bath area. But, the best part of our bath area is that we use the back of the door to mark the boys' heights as they grow up. It brings a smile to my heart every time I reflect on how little they were the last time I measured them and to see how much they have grown.

Is there anything special about your bath area? (Reflect on something unique in your bath area; something that others don't have, or aren't able to do.)

_____

_____

_____

_____

As I have said several times before, sunlight is the key to how you feel in any given space. In the bath area, morning sun is a great start to the day. In the evening, the setting sun sets the mood for romance and begins the period of restoring the energy spent that day.

How is the daylight in your bath area? Too much or too little?

_____

_____

_____

_____

_____

Are there dramatic differences in your bath area between the morning and evening sunlight? How so?

_____

_____

_____

_____

_____

How does the sun's effect on your bath area make you feel in the summer versus the winter?

_____

_____

_____

_____

_____

_____

"The light which puts out our eyes is darkness to us.

Only that day dawns to which we are awake.

There is more day to dawn. The sun is but a morning star."

Henry David Thoreau

What are you most thankful for about **your** bath area?

_____

_____

_____

_____

_____

_____

_____

the
guest room...

In this segment of *...experiencing home...* we are taking a bit of a detour. Rather than focusing on your own experiences, we are going to think through what others experience, or what you hope they will experience as guests in your home.

The guest room is the place where others stay when they visit your home. Whether their intentions are to spend time with you for an extended period or just to stop over on their way elsewhere, they are looking for a place for their body to rest and rejuvenate. We all recognize that when we stay in someone else's home the experience won't be as comfortable as it would be in our own home. But as the host, why not attempt to make the experience as wonderful as possible for those who visit? A valuable tool for this attempt might be to explore some of your own past experiences.

"Offer hospitality to one another without grumbling.
Each one should use whatever gift he has received to
serve others, faithfully administering God's grace in its various forms."

1 Peter 4:9-10

Outside of your own home, of course, think through some of the most memorable places you have stayed. What did you like about them?

_____

_____

_____

_____

Was it the beauty, the size, the amenities, the location or did it just feel like home?

_____

_____

_____

_____

What do you remember seeing, feeling, smelling in those places?

_____

_____

_____

_____

What were some of the experiences you had there?

_____

_____

_____

_____

_____

Do you think your guests want to return and stay in your guest room? Why or why not?

_____

_____

_____

_____

"One should always sleep in all of one's guest beds,

to make sure that they are comfortable."

Eleanor Roosevelt

Do your guests only sleep in the guest room, or do they go there to nap or read a book? Why or why not?

_____

_____

_____

_____

How do you think your guests feel when spending time in your guest room?

_____

_____

_____

What do they smell, feel and hear?

_____

_____

_____

_____

What experience do you want your guests to have?

_____

_____

_____

_____

_____

_____

Again, I want to take a moment and mention the importance

for you to not feel the need to go out and buy a bunch

of stuff for your guest room. But instead, what can you alter

about the way your guests experience your guest room?

Maybe it's removing all of the "storage" stuff in the closet,

opening the drapes when they enter, or

maybe it's a matter of giving them your room.

What are you most thankful for about your guest room?

_____

_____

_____

_____

_____

_____

_____

_____

_____

_____

_____

_____

What do you think your guests are most thankful for about your guest room?

_____

_____

_____

_____

_____

_____

_____

_____

_____

_____

_____

the
attic...

Do you have an attic that has stairs or a ladder up to it and is one in which you can walk around? I don't. Whether or not you do pretty much depends on when your house was built. Before the 1950's, most homes were built board-by-board, including the roof and ceiling. This creates the large wide-open space between the roof and the ceiling. More recent construction methods use trusses, which are the large, web-like (triangular), pieces that make up the roof, the ceiling and the structural elements all in one. Because of the webbing, the attic space is lost. Some parts of the country and certain craftsmen still build board-by-board when timing isn't the driving factor.

This discussion is directed towards those of you with that large open space up in your attic. However, if you don't have one, you may be able to apply these questions to spaces like the storage area in a basement, or a detached storage building. My attic is about 140 degrees in the summer and full of black, itchy insulation so I miss out on this one.

The attic seems to have a significant connection to history. How many movies can you think of that have a scene in an attic, with someone looking through old items of historical significance? Attics are usually storage areas, but are sometimes finished for additional living space.

"Being 'contented' ought to mean in English, as it does in French, being pleased. Being content with an attic ought not to mean being unable to move from it and resigned to living in it; it ought to mean appreciating all there is in such a position."

Gilbert K. Chesterton

How does your attic feel to you? Scary, exciting, dirty? Describe it.

_____

_____

_____

_____

_____

_____

Does your attic have any natural light? If it has one little window (like many do), cover the window with something and describe the difference. How does the light change your experience?

_____

_____

_____

_____

_____

Is there any significance to your attic? (Maybe your home has been handed down from generation to generation.)

_____

_____

_____

_____

_____

_____

_____

What kinds of things are in your attic? Anything of significance, or just junk?

_____

_____

_____

_____

_____

_____

Pick out an item or two and reflect on its history. Why do you still keep it?

_____

_____

_____

_____

_____

_____

If your attic is finished as living space, who likes to use it? Why?

_____

_____

_____

_____

_____

What are you most thankful for **about** your attic? Or even what you're most thankful for **in** your attic.

_____

_____

_____

_____

_____

the
garage...

Despite all of the things garages can be used for, it seems to me that the basis for their existence is similar in almost all cases: storage. We store cars, bikes, boats, boxes, bins, tools, and anything else you can think of, quite frankly. As I design homes, the three-car garage seems to be a given for larger homes even though most people only have two cars. When I ask them why they need three the overriding concern is storage.

However, garages are not just for storage anymore, but for recreation and hobbies. The older, more stereotypical hobbies include woodworking and car rebuilding, but people are beginning to take it to the next level. I have clients asking for the garage to be tall enough for indoor basketball, long enough to practice archery, or wide enough for boats, campers or any multitude of toys. I've even designed a garage that allows for a pitcher's mound to be rolled in and attached to the floor to allow my client's son to practice his pitching in the winter.

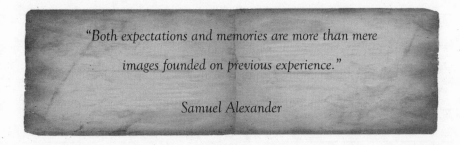

"Both expectations and memories are more than mere images founded on previous experience."

Samuel Alexander

As you sit in your garage, what do you see? Make a general list of all the stuff in your garage.

_____   _____

_____   _____

_____   _____

_____   _____

_____   _____

_____   _____

_____   _____

Now, think about the garage of your childhood home. What things were in that garage that are not in your present garage?

_____   _____

_____   _____

_____   _____

_____   _____

_____   _____

What kinds of things did you do in your garage growing up?

_____

_____

_____

_____

What kinds of things do you do now in your own garage? Which is your favorite thing to do?

_____

_____

_____

_____

I believe that for many of us men, the garage is also a place for learning and instruction from our fathers, uncles or friends. Sometimes we've even learned things the hard way, hopefully without burning anything down or cutting anything off. Whether it's caring for an engine or using power tools, we all seem to have learned some life skill in the garage. My father never really taught me a thing about cars, but he did teach me a lot about power tools and basic woodworking. As times change, more women are changing the oil in the car and fixing their own bicycles. Nevertheless, we all have different experiences within our garages. I clean ours and make sure everything is in its place so the car will fit. My wife Elisha walks through our garage. During bad weather my boys use the garage for riding their scooters around in circles.

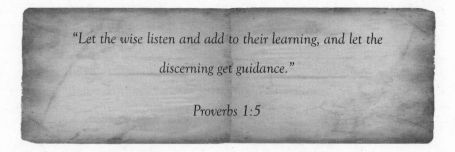

"Let the wise listen and add to their learning, and let the discerning get guidance."

Proverbs 1:5

What things did you learn in your childhood garage?

_____

_____

_____

_____

_____

_____

What things have you taught, or do you plan to teach in your garage?

_____

_____

_____

_____

The garage also seems to be a place of escape. We all need time alone; time to focus on the things we enjoy. For many men, that place is the garage.

"As homeowners shared their biggest gripes about their home, some key findings bubbled up to the surface. Among them, that even members of close-knit families crave alone time."

Unknown

Where is your place of escape? Why?

_____

_____

_____

_____

_____

What do you like to do when you escape?

_____

_____

_____

_____

_____

_____

_____

What are you most thankful for in your garage?

_____

_____

_____

_____

_____

_____

_____

_____

_____

_____

_____

_____

the
backyard...

Unlike most of the spaces of your home, backyards are unique and there are no two alike. You may have the exact same floor plan as others on your street, but odds are your backyards are different. Our backyards look and perform very differently for each and every one of us. You may have a beautiful flower garden, a fire pit, a dog run, a tire swing or even a golf course in your backyard. Either way, you have chosen and set up your backyard according to your desires and your hobbies.

As you sit near your house and look at your backyard, describe what you see.

_____

_____

_____

Now move to the edge of your back yard, looking back at your house and change your perspective. What do you see differently?

_____

_____

_____

_____

What things were in your backyard when you arrived, and what have you changed?

_____

_____

_____

_____

What do you most enjoy doing in your backyard?

_____

_____

_____

_____

How about the rest of your family, what do they enjoy most?

_____

_____

_____

_____

_____

The great part about our yards is that we have our Creator doing the decorating.

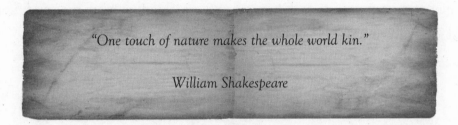

"One touch of nature makes the whole world kin."

William Shakespeare

Now describe the pleasurable sights, smells and even sounds in your backyard.

_____

_____

_____

_____

_____

Enjoying the warmth of the sunlight, the romance of the moonlight, and the calming effect of the fresh air are all great ways to experience your home. Outdoor living has become a critical part of the way we live. Outdoor furniture is becoming more and more like our indoor furniture. Outdoor kitchens and televisions are providing the means for entertaining outside as easily as one might entertain inside. Space heaters and fireplaces now allow for spending time outside, in spite of the temperatures. Ultimately, we are spending more time and money outdoors than ever before.

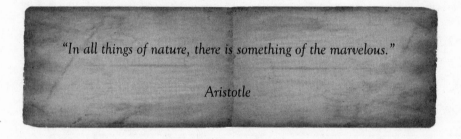

"In all things of nature, there is something of the marvelous."

Aristotle

What activities can you do in your backyard that are different than anywhere else in your home?

_____

_____

_____

_____

Once again, reflect on one of your childhood backyards. What makes it so memorable?

_____

_____

_____

_____

_____

_____

What are you most thankful for in your backyard?

_____

_____

_____

_____

_____

_____

_____

the
others...

What other spaces did I forget, or, what other spaces do you have that you wish I had covered? Well, rather than my continuing this book forever and ever with spaces like the exercise room, your child's room, or the pantry, I thought I might call it good.

Feel free to take it beyond a given space or room. Maybe a chair or a window seat is the spot you prefer to focus on. There might be a certain tree you like to sit under where you most prefer to reflect, pray or even worship.

> *"Stress levels are higher and higher, and people are hibernating in their homes. They're using their home more and finding a lot of comfort there. So they're figuring what is most important in their lives and creating spaces that offer a better quality of life—creating a sense of escape inside their homes."*
>
> *Unknown*

As you settle into any given space or spot continue to use the general prompts and questions you've seen so far:

- Describe what you see. (Don't forget to look from another perspective as well.)

- What do you see, hear, smell or feel?

- What effect does the sun have?

- Reflect on a time when...

Or even some fun questions as well, like:

- What relationships exist in this room? Who uses it? Why does that matter?

- What spaces do your pets like?

- Are there any plants in the room? What effect do they have on your mood?

- Do you use this space for what it was initially designed for?

- What is the best nesting spot within this space?

- Does your personality change from room to room?

And don't forget the most important question:

- What are you most thankful for?

the
next day...

Now that you've completed the list of spaces I provided and any other spaces you might have chosen to experience, what do you do now? What about the next day, and the one after that? How do you take these experiences into your everyday way-of-life? How do you keep the experiences going?

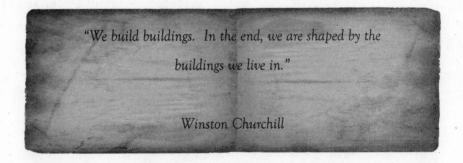

"We build buildings. In the end, we are shaped by the buildings we live in."

Winston Churchill

Here are a number of general ideas that may assist you in continuing this journey beyond today. First, try having the experience in different places, in different chairs or seats. For example, if you typically read a book in your bed, try sitting on the floor of your front porch. Second, look for different types of light, particularly sunlight. When you'd like to take a nap, try lying down on the floor in the middle of a sunbeam. It might just be the perfect spot. Third, attempt to create a mood. If you want to have a nice day of reflection on your childhood, bake some cookies and watch some cartoons. Lastly, invite someone over to join you. It doesn't need to be a large gathering, maybe just a friend or two. Let them experience your home with you. When friends come over, slip off their shoes and curl up on your sofa, take it as a compliment. They're ready to enjoy their time with you, to have an experience with you. This is not an exhaustive list, but just a few ideas. Always keep in mind that varying places at different times of the day will definitely allow for a variety of experiences.

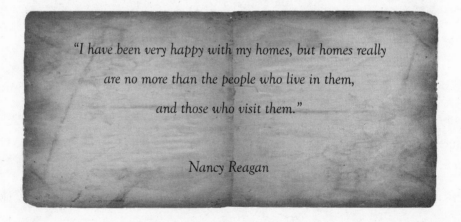

"I have been very happy with my homes, but homes really are no more than the people who live in them, and those who visit them."

Nancy Reagan

After all of this, you might also be asking yourself, "How do I improve my experiences in my study, or my kitchen, etc.?" Remember, the goal of this book is not to urge you to remodel or get a home makeover, but you have a fair question here. Let me ask you, what kinds of experiences do you want to have? What kinds of experiences do you want others to have? As you think through the rooms and spaces you have been journaling about, are there one or two things you could do to one of the spaces to allow for a better experience next time?

Earlier on I mentioned the importance of the five senses. A general suggestion for improving your experiences would be to focus on your senses. Attempt to alter the things that will have the greatest appeal to your senses.

For example:

- **Your sense of sight-** Change your pictures around or put up some new ones. Change the light bulbs in your lamps to a softer type of light. Change the colors on your walls.

Your final Design 101: Colors

Red- Implies strength, power; raises your blood pressure.

Orange- Signifies creativity, success; increases

oxygen to your brain.

Yellow- Implies joy, energy; associated with food.

Green- Implies nature, growth; the most restful

color to the human eye.

Blue- Signifies trust, wisdom; typically produces a calming effect.

Purple- For nobility, luxury and appeals to children.

White- Implies light, purity; usually has a positive connotation.

Black- Is formal, mysterious; creates aggression.

- **Your sense of smell**- Use a new air freshener, change to scented candles, or take out your trash more often.

- **Your sense of hearing-** Use more music as background noise or open your windows to listen to the outdoors.

- **Your sense of touch-** Get some softer blankets and pillows or put up your feet more often.

- **Your sense of taste-** Enjoy your favorite drink when hanging out by the fireplace or soaking in the tub.

Here are a few specific things you may like to try to improve your everyday experiences:

- Place a chair on your front porch, even though it may not fit perfectly, that calls your name when the sprinklers are running.

- Hang your wedding photo or high school picture on the wall in your entryway.

- Have your child read a book in your study while you work one evening.

- Set a puzzle out on the coffee table in the living room that's just begging for someone to sit down and put a few pieces in place.

- Have candles sitting in the center of your dining table rather than salt and pepper shakers.

- A more drastic idea may be cutting a hole in the south wall of your kitchen to allow for a window instead of a cabinet that is presently there.

- In your play area, post pictures of friends that you have spent special time with.

- How about placing your wedding photo album on your dresser in your bedroom?

- Next time you have twenty minutes free, go take a hot shower, soak up the steam, and take a deep breath.

- For your guests, put a chocolate on the pillow and give them better towels than yours.

- Start collecting things of historical significance for your family and place them in your attic or storage space, ultimately creating a future experience for generations to come.

- For your garage it's pretty simple: go teach your son how to change the oil or your daughter how to pump up a bike tire.

- Hang up a hammock or a bird feeder in your back yard.

"Many of us concentrate on the bigger picture, but everyday pleasures are often to be found in the details."

Jane Burden, The Complete Home

I hope some of these ideas help stir in you other ideas for having the experiences you want to have in your home. The important thing to remember is that the discovery of experiences in your home is ongoing. Always keep looking for and creating ways to have great experiences in your home.

My guide through your home is nearing completion. But, there is one last thing I want you to reflect on. Even though we can experience joy in our homes, it is not complete joy. How can you discover the real, complete, unprecedented and unfathomable joy that God intends for you?

The next chapter will explain, read on...

"In my Father's house are many rooms; if it were not so, I would have told you. I am going there to prepare a place for you."

John 14:2

THE
HOME...

Do you remember some of the clichés I mentioned earlier? Phrases like, "Home is where the heart is," "There's no place like home," "Home sweet home." For some reason or another we hold onto and believe in these clichés. Why? We have been created in the image of God and because of that, we have an ingrained desire to be at HOME with Him.

God desires to experience His HOME, THE HOME, *with you.*

We find great joy in experiencing our homes, the kind of joy that's special to hold on to and remember. However, no matter how much we change our homes or what experiences we have in them, the joy we experience at home is limited. Even though we can experience a more powerful and fulfilling joy right now, we will never experience the real, complete, and deeply satisfying joy that God intends for us unless we have a personal relationship with Him. Through this relationship

God provides the contentment our hearts long for, the meaning for our lives we search for, the peace we all hope for and, of course, the joy that each of us desires; the joy that each and every one of us desires is found there, at HOME with God.

> *"For we know that if the earthly tent which is our house is torn down, we have a building from God, a house not made with hands, eternal in the heavens."*
>
> *The Apostle Paul, II Corinthians 5:1*

The HOME I am referring to is eternity with God. You know what the beautiful part is? Eternity with God can begin right now. You can begin to have more fulfilling and joyful experiences today. How's that, you ask? How can I begin to have more joyful experiences in my home? And, how do I go about experiencing God's HOME with Him eternally? Jesus Christ says in John 14:6,

"I am the way and the truth and the life. No one comes to the Father except through me." So, to answer your question, to experience a relationship with God we must know Jesus Christ, His Son, personally.

In order to know Jesus Christ personally, we must come to understand and accept a few critical things first.

First, we all have sinned. The Bible tells us in Romans 3:23, *"All have sinned and fall short of the Glory of God."* At some point in our lives, we have done at least one thing that displeases God. That one time (let alone the countless other times) makes us a 'sinner', just like stealing a pack gum makes someone a thief.

Second, God is loving and full of grace. I think most of us believe that. But, the same Bible that tells us that God is loving also tells us that He is equally just. James 2:19 says, *"He will by no means let the guilty go unpunished."* We are told in Hebrews 9:27, *"Just as man is destined to die once, and after that to face judgment."* There is no denying the fact that all of our actions will be judged by the God that must be just.

Third, Jesus Christ is both God and Man as we are told in John 1:1,14, *"In the beginning was the Word, and the Word was with God, and was God, and became flesh... and dwelt among us."* Therefore, Jesus is the only human able to pay for all of our sins. He did so on the cross. His life, death and resurrection give us the proof of God's desire to have us with Him.

Understanding the previous points you have just read is one thing, but accepting them as absolute truth is the critical part. This is called faith. We all have faith in something. For example, I have faith that the sun will rise, that my truck will start and that my wife, Elisha, will always love me. But to express that faith, I must accept it, trust in it, live my life with it, and in the case of my wife reciprocate it. Another example of utilizing our faith is when we receive a gift. We accept the gift in faith as something given to us without the assumption of needing to work or pay for it. Ephesians 2:8-9 says that, *"For it is by grace you have been saved, through faith - and this not from yourselves, it is a gift of God - not by works, so that no one can boast."*

> *"I have told you this so that my joy may be in you and*
>
> *that your joy may be complete."*
>
> Jesus of Nazareth, John 15:11

This offer from God to experience joy in the ultimate HOME and more fully here on earth in our homes is an amazing gift. A gift we don't deserve, but get to enjoy. A gift we can't work for or earn, but should be thankful for. Just like I can't work for the sun to come up, and I can't work for Elisha's love, I just accept it as I would any other gift. Most importantly, we can't earn the gift God gives us. We can't work for His grace or His willingness to forgive us for our sins.

If these last few words are new to you, and you would like to experience the ultimate HOME in the presence of God, ask God in prayer to forgive all of the sins you have committed. Then accept His forgiveness and relationship offer by faith.

Here is a sample prayer to help you:

Father God, I recognize that I am a sinner and that you
are a just God that cannot look past my sin. I accept the fact
that your Son, Jesus Christ, died on the cross for me personally.
I understand that I am unworthy to receive the gift Jesus
provided and I recognize that I can not work enough to earn it.
I accept your gift through faith. Thank you Father for saving me.
In Jesus' name...Amen.

If this is a prayer that you truly feel in your heart, God knows, and the angels are singing. Jesus says in Revelation 3:20, *"Here I am! I stand at the door and knock. If anyone hears my voice and opens the door, I will come in and eat with him, and he with me."* He wishes to join you... join you in EXPERIENCING HOME.

If you wish to investigate further resources about this topic, please view the following chapter, "the sources."

the
sources...

Resources available for those needing assistance in dealing with bad childhood experiences:

Printed:

Holy Bible: New International Version, NIV. Zondervan Publishing.

Total Forgiveness. R.T. Kendall. Charisma House.

When You've Been Wronged. Erwin W. Lutzer. Moody Publishers

The Wounded Heart: Hope for Adult Victims of Childhood Sexual Abuse. Dr. Dan B. Allender. Navpress.

Websites:

www.aacc.net   American Association of Christian Counselors

www.newlife.com   New Life Ministries

www.focusonthefamily.com   Focus on the Family

Resources available for those searching for more answers about the person of Jesus Christ:

Printed:

Holy Bible: New International Version, NIV. Zondervan Publishing.

The Case for Christ. Lee Strobel. Zondervan Publishing

The Case for Faith. Lee Strobel. Zondervan Publishing

More than a Carpenter. Josh McDowell. Living Books

The Purpose Driven Life: What on Earth Am I Here For? Rick Warren. Zondervan Publishing

Websites:

www.eeinternational.org
      Press the "Step to Life" button

www.purposedrivenlife.com
      Press the "Who is Jesus" button

www.leestrobel.com
      Look under the "Video Channels" tab

www.josh.org
      Look under the "Resources" tab

The books that were commonly quoted from in this book.

The Comfortable Home, Jane Burden. Ryland, Peters and Small Publishing.

Finding Home: An Important Path to Faith and Family, Jim Daly.
David C. Cook Publishing.

Holy Bible: New International Version, NIV. Zondervan Publishing.

House Thinking: A Room-by-Room Look at How We Live, Winifred Gallagher.
Harper Collins Publishing.

Pottery Barn: Home. Oxmoor House Publishing.

Contact information for back cover testimonials.

Vince D'Acchioli, On Target Ministries
    www.ontargetinstitute.org
    1-719-481-2620

Natalie Lewis, Featured ReDesigner on HDTV
    LewisStyle Franchising President/Founder
    www.LewisStyle.com
    1-800-627-2711

This book available for purchase at

www.experiencingyourhome.com